MINNICH FUNERAL HOME
415 East Wilson Boulevard
Hagerstown, Maryland 21740

Presented to

_____

_____

by

_____

_____

date

_____

Harvest
of
Hope

CLINTON T. HOWELL

THOMAS NELSON INC., PUBLISHERS
Nashville • New York

Acknowledgment

It is the editor's belief that the necessary permissions from authors of the selections herein or their authorized agents have been obtained. In the event of any question arising as to the use of any selection, the editor, while expressing regret for any error he unconsciously made, will be pleased to make the necessary arrangement and correction in future editions of this book.

The editor has also made every effort to trace the authorship of all selections. When no name appears the authorship is unknown.

Contents

God give me hills to climb
And strength for the climbing

—Arthur Guiterman

Preface

THE SELECTED POEMS and talks in this volume have been called the "literature of power" in their strength to guide, encourage, and inspire persons in the battle for successful living.

These heart-to-heart talks cover every subject faced by the wayfaring pilgrim in this life's earthly journey.

The book offers special appeal and guidance to the aimless, the discouraged, the despairing, the despondent; and seeks to raise to honorable proportions the wholesome aims and worthy ambitions of the otherwise defeated ones.

Here is fresh admonition and new courage for the young and not so young who are snared by feelings of failure—to hold on, to rise, to fight again, and win. It seeks to remind those whose feelings of inferiority or inadequacy are hindering their full potential that there are about them doors, ways, means, and opportunities to be entered, seized, used.

The aim of this volume is to show you a way, a plan, a grand design for making of yours a good, great, and noble life—altogether fruitful and satisfying.

Clinton T. Howell

Don't Quit

When things go wrong, as they sometimes will,
When the road you're trudging seems all up hill,
When the funds are low and the debts are high,
And you want to smile, but you have to sigh,
When care is pressing you down a bit,
Rest, if you must—but don't you quit.

Life is queer with its twists and turns,
As everyone of us sometimes learns,
And many a failure turns about
When he might have won had he stuck it out;
Don't give up, though the pace seems slow—
You might succeed with another blow.

Often the goal is nearer than
It seems to a faint and faltering man,
Often the struggler has given up
When he might have captured the victor's cup.
And he learned too late, when the night slipped down,
How close he was to the golden crown.

Success is failure turned inside out—
The silver tint of the clouds of doubt—
And you never can tell how close you are,
It may be near when it seems afar;
So stick to the fight when you're hardest hit—
It's when things seem worst that you mustn't quit.

—Edgar A. Guest

KEEP A-GOIN'

If you strike a thorn or rose,
  Keep a-goin'!
If it hails or if it snows,
  Keep a-goin'!
'Taint no use to sit an' whine
When the fish ain't on your line;
Bait your hook an' keep a-tryin'—
  Keep a-goin'!

When the weather kills your crop,
  Keep a-goin'!
Though 'tis work to reach the top,
  Keep a-goin'!
S'pose you're out o' ev'ry dime,
Gittin' broke ain't any crime;
Tell the world you're feelin' *prime*—
  Keep a-goin'!

When it looks like all is up,
  Keep a-goin'!
Drain the sweetness from the cup,
  Keep a-goin'!
See the wild birds on the wing,
Hear the bells that sweetly ring,
When you feel like sighin', sing—
  Keep a-goin'!

—*Frank L. Stanton*

TO THE QUITTER

The world won't care if you quit
And the world won't whine if you fail;
The busy world won't notice it,
No matter how loudly you wail.

Nobody will worry that you
Have relinquished the fight and gone
    down
For it's only the things that you do
That are worth while and get your
    renown.

The quitters are quickly forgot;
On them the world spends little time;
And a few e'er care that you've not
The courage or patience to climb.

So give up and quit in despair,
And take your place back on the shelf;
But don't think the world's going
    to care;
You are injuring only yourself.

—Author Unknown

IF IT'S WORTH WHILE

If it's worth while, then it's worth a few blows,
    Worth a few setbacks and worth a few bruises;
If it's worth while—and it is, I suppose—
    It's worth keeping on, though the first struggle
    loses.

If it's worth while, then it's worth a good fight,
    Worth a few bouts with the demon, Disaster,
Worth going after with courage and might,
    Worth keeping on till you've proved you are
    master.

If it's worth while, then it's worth a few pains,
    Worth a few heartaches and worth a few sor-
    rows,
Worth clinging fast to the hope that remains,
    Worth going on through the doubtful tomor-
    rows.

Stand to the battle and see the test through,
    Pay all you have in endurance and might for
    it;
If it's worth while and a good thing to do,
    Then it is worth all it costs in the fight for it.

—Edgar A. Guest

BE STRONG

Be strong!
We are not here to play, to dream, to drift;
We have hard work to do, and loads to lift;
Shun not the struggle—face it; 'tis God's gift.

Be strong!
Say not, "The days are evil. Who's to blame?"
And fold the hands and acquiesce—oh shame!
Stand up, speak out, and bravely, in God's name.

Be strong!
It matters not how deep intrenched the wrong,
How hard the battle goes, the day how long;
Faint not—fight on! Tomorrow comes the song.

—*Maltbie Davenport Babcock*

Baseball was my whole life and I loved it. When my knees finally went and I realized I had to get out of the game, I thought it was the end of the world. But I began to discover it really wasn't the end of *the* world at all; it was just the end of *a* world. There's a lot of worlds out there, and you kinda gotta take what you're offered and make the best of it.

—*Mickey Mantle*

God's Whisper

"Anybody might have heard it, but God's whisper came to me," says the poet.

God always whispers. At least to the soul. He may thunder to nations and speak to armies in the lightning. But to the individual His message is not in the mighty wind, nor the earthquake, nor the fire, but in the still small voice.

God lives in the bottom of the funnel of silence. He is the treasure concealed in solitude. He meets men alone, in the dark. Congregations have their use, and books, and papers, and multitudes, and friends, but God loves the silent way.

He is every soul's most secret secret. If, as Thoreau said, it takes two to tell the truth; it also takes two to make a revelation; it takes the whisper of God and the listening of man.

God's whisper runs to and fro upon the earth. It might be heard in all cottages, palaces, marts, offices, inns, and councils—if only we listened.

Go into the silence. Give your souls time to calm. Let the hurly-burly die down, the crash of passion, the struggle of doubt, the pain of failure, the ranklings of wrong, the clamor of ambition. Cease from self. Be still.

Practice this. It is an art, and not to be mastered out of hand. Try it again and again, as patiently, as determinedly, as lovingly as one practices the violin or the making of a statue.

And after awhile, as virtuosity comes after long trials,

there will come to life in you the needed sixth sense, by which you can hear the whisper.

Some day you will get it. It may rise like a strange dawn in your consciousness. It may stir in you as life stirs in the egg. It may pentrate the deep chambers of your being as a strain of mystic music.

And it will be the prize of life. You will not be able to give it to another. Every man must receive such things himself. All of God's most vital secrets are marked nontransferable.

But it will be yours—that which in all your life is most utterly yours. It will strengthen you in weakness, cheer you in hours of gloom. When you are at sea and confused, lost in the winds of casuistry, it will shine out as a pole-star. When you are afraid it will reinforce you as an army with banners.

It will lull you to sleep with its music. It will give you poise. It will give you decision. No man can tell what the whisper says. Each soul must hear for itself. This is a great secret. One can only point the way—the way to silence.

There stands God and says: "I will give to eat of the hidden manna, and will give him a white stone, and in the stone a new name written, which no man knoweth saving he that receiveth it. He that hath an ear, let him hear what the Spirit saith."

THE SECRET

I met God in the morning
  When my day was at its best,
And His presence came like sunrise,
  Like a glory in my breast.

All day long the Presence lingered,
  All day long He stayed with me,
And we sailed in perfect calmness
  O'er a very troubled sea.

Other ships were blown and battered,
  Other ships were sore distressed,
But the winds that seemed to drive them
  Brought to us a peace and rest.

Then I thought of other mornings,
  With a keen remorse of mind,
When I too had loosed the moorings,
  With the Presence left behind.

So I think I know the secret,
  Learned from many a troubled way:
You must seek Him in the morning
  If you want Him through the day!

—Ralph Spaulding Cushman

Don't Run Out

Everyone needs someone to love, some exciting labor, and something to live for.

You sometimes wish you could chuck it all and get lost—just give up and run away. The extreme of this feeling is thoughts of suicide, or a turn to alcohol or other drugs—the coward's way of solution—which solves nothing, but establishes hurt, disappointment, and sorrow.

This seldom temptation comes to many of us along the way. 'Tis the way of ignominy and shame. Stand up to life—don't entertain even the inclination to run out on it.

Try to understand the factors seeking your final defeat. Anxiety, depression, poor marital relationships are some; anger, frustration, and guilt are others. All are more dangerous than poisionous plants and reptiles.

When you're tempted to do some drastic thing you are caught in deep emotional conflict, due, for the most part, to seemingly uncontrollable environmental factors.

The recognition and prevention of a suicide pattern requires outside help. Get hold of yourself—expose the event or issue; recognize the reason. Talk it out with a friend, relative, or counselor. Plain talk is a great pressure valve. You may gain enough insight to realize all is not lost, that there are solutions at hand and ways ahead and those who care.

The sum of the whole matter is that our intelligence and our affections are our most dependable bulwarks against self-destruction. To recognize such a force within us is the first step toward its control.

Don't despair—refuse to run out; the future is a great land, and has no end.

Life is a warfare; and he who easily desponds deserts a double duty—he betrays the noblest property of man, which is dauntless resolution; and he rejects the providence of that all-gracious Being who guides and rules the universe.

—*Jane Porter*

Despair is like forward children, who, when you take away one of their playthings, throw the rest into the fire for madness. It grows angry with itself, turns its own executioner, and revenges its misfortunes on its own head.

—*Charron*

I am one of those lucky fellows who inherited a fortune. It came, after years of poverty and reckless living, as the result of a death I had no cause to regret. The man who bequeathed riches to me was my former self. He died of selfishness, pessimism, fear, worry, vain regrets, envy.

—*Vash Young*

What a difference it makes when we are using life rather than having life use us. When we, to a marked degree, are managing our moods, controlling our emotions, making life meaningful, filling every day with the heights of Christian living, we may say with confidence that we are using life.

But when worry grips the mind and paralyzes the heart, or the dull edge of sin robs life of radiancy, or fear grips our life, rather than an abiding faith, and life runs out into a morass of doubt, disillusionment, and despair, we know that life is using us.

—Frank A. Court

Guns aren't lawful;
Nooses give;
Gas smells awful;
You might as well live.

—Dorothy Parker

He knows, He loves, He cares;
Nothing this truth can dim.
He gives the very best to those
Who leave the choice with Him.

—Author Unknown

THE END OF THE ROPE

When you've lost every vestige of hope
And you think you are beaten and done,
When you've come to the end of your rope,
Tie a knot in the end and hang on.

Have courage; for here is the dope;
When you stand with your back to the wall,
Though you've come to the end of your rope
Tie a knot in the end and hang on.

Don't admit that life's getting your goat
When your friends seem to all disappear,
When you've come to the end of your rope,
Tie a knot in the end and hang on.

—Margaret Nickerson Martin

RISKY BUSINESS

It's a risk to have a husband; a risk to have
    a son:
A risk to pour your confidences out to
    anyone;
A risk to pick a daisy, for there's sure to
    be a cop;
A risk to go on living, but a greater risk
    to stop.

—Ruth Mason Rice

In the lottery of life there are more prizes drawn than blanks, and to one misfortune there are fifty advantages. Despondency is the most unprofitable feeling a man can indulge in.

—DeWitt Talmage

Nothing to live for? Soul, that cannot be,
Though when hearts break, the world seems
emptiness;
But unto thee I bring in thy distress
A message, born of love and sympathy,
And it may prove, O soul, the golden key
To all things beautiful and good, and bless

Thy life which looks to thee so comfortless!
This is the word: "Some one hath need of
    thee."

—Emma C. Down

To put yourself in the second place is the whole significance of life.

—Richard Roberts

DON'T GIVE UP

"Twixt failure and success the point's so fine
Men sometimes know not when they touch the line.
Just when the pearl was waiting one more plunge,
How many a struggler has thrown up the sponge!
Then take this honey from the bitterest cup:
"There is no failure save in giving up!"

—Author Unknown

If we might have a second chance
　　To live the days once more,
And rectify mistakes we've made
　　To even up the score.
If we might have a second chance
　　To use the knowledge gained,
Perhaps we might become at last
　　As fine as God ordained.
But though we can't retrace our steps
　　However, stands the score,
Tomorrow brings another chance
　　For us to try once more.

—Farr

THE SENSIBLE WAY

There's nothing so bad
  That it could not be worse;
There's little that time may not mend,
  And troubles, no matter how thickly
    they come,
Most surely will come to an end.

You've stumbled—well so have we all in
  our time.
Don't dwell over much on regret,
For you're sorry, God knows, we'll leave
  it at that
Let past things be past, and forget.

Don't despond, don't give up, but just be
  yourself—
The self that is highest and best,
Just live every day in a sensible way,
And then leave to God all the rest.

—Author Unknown

You need to learn to work with yourself,
to use your will power on the side of yourself.

—Author Unknown

THANATOPSIS

So live that when thy summons comes to join
The innumerable caravan which moves
To that mysterious realm where each shall take
His chamber in the silent halls of death,
Thou go not, like the quarry-slave at night,
Scourged to his dungeon, but, sustained and soothed
By an unfaltering trust, approach thy grave
Like one who wraps the drapery of his couch
About him, and lies down to pleasant dreams.

—William Cullen Bryant

From IS LIFE WORTH LIVING!

Is life worth living? Yes, so long
   As there is wrong to right,
Wail of the weak against the strong,
   Or tyranny to fight;
Long as there lingers gloom to chase,
   Or streaming tear to dry,
One kindred woe, one sorrowing face
   That smiles as we draw nigh;
Long as a tale of anguish swells
The heart, and lids grow wet,
And at the sound of Christmas bells
   We pardon and forget;
So long as Faith with Freedom reigns,
   And loyal Hope survives,
And gracious Charity remains
   To leaven lowly lives;
While there is one untrodden tract
   For Intellect or Will,
And men are free to think and act
   Life is worth living still.

—Alfred Austin

Life is a flower of which love is the honey.

—Victor Hugo

TIME

So the sands of Time that
    slowly flow
From out my hour glass
Will all too soon have ebbed
    away,
    My life will then be past.
So I must make the most of
    time
    And drift not with the tide,
For killing time's not
    murder,
    It's more like suicide.

—Author Unknown

Let no man write
Thy epitaph, Emmett; thou shalt not go
Without thy funeral strain! O young and good,
And wise, though erring here, thou shalt not go
Unhonored or unsung. And better thus
Beneath that undiscriminating stroke,
Better to fall, than to have lived to mourn,
As sure thou wouldst, in misery and remorse,
Thine own disastrous triumph****
How happier thus, in that heroic mood
That takes away the sting of death, to die,
By all the good and all the wise forgiven!
Yea, in all ages by the wise and good
To be remembered, mourned, and honored still!

—Southey to Robert Emmett

You
don't
become
a mistake
just
because
you
have
made
one.

WHAT I NEED

I need a strength to keep me true
And straight in everything I do;
I need a power to keep me strong
When I am tempted to do wrong;
I need a grace to keep me pure
When passion tries its deadly lure;
I need a love to keep me sweet
When hardness and mistrust I meet;
I need an arm to be my stay
When dark with trouble grows my day:
And naught on earth can these afford,
But all is found in Christ my Lord.

—Theodore Horton

BEGIN AGAIN

Every day is a fresh beginning,
   Every morn is the world made new.
You who are weary of sorrow and sinning,
   Here is a beautiful hope for you,—
   A hope for me and a hope for you.

Every day is a fresh beginning;
   Listen, my soul, to the glad refrain,
And, spite of old sorrow and older sinning,
   And puzzles forecasted and possible pain,
   Take heart with the day, and begin again.

—Susan Coolidge

Make me too brave to lie or be unkind.
Make me too understanding, too, to mind
The little hurts companions give, and
   friends,
The careless hurts that no one quite
   intends.
May I forget
What ought to be forgotten, and recall,
Unfailing, all
That ought to be recalled, each kindly
   thing,
Forgetting what might sting.
To all upon my way,
Day after day,
Let me be joy, be hope! Let my life sing!

—Davies

Accept Yourself

Self-rejection is a liability. Self-acceptance is an asset. Yet it is easy to give up before a good self-analysis is made.

See your limitations, but keep your mind on your strong points and build them. If you are physically crippled, learn from others what they do for this kind of handicap.

Search for new ways to overcome discouragement and go on to victory. If you are pushed back, stop and seek a way to push through the next time. Summon your courage, believe in your powers, and have confidence that you will not be defeated, except by circumstances over which you have no control.

Overcome pessimism by bringing optimism to the front that you will win and you will have more power. "Nerve up with affirmatives," urged Ralph Waldo Emerson. "Don't waste yourself in rejection, nor bark against the bad, but chant the beauty of the good." Don't defeat your purposes and weaken your chances of success and happiness by easy self-rejection.

> You cannot run away from a
> weakness; you must sometime fight
> it out or perish. And if that be so,
> why not now, and where you stand?
>
> —*Robert Louis Stevenson*

MYSELF

I have to live with myself, and so
I want to be fit for myself to know,
I want to be able, as the days go by,
Always to look myself straight in the eye;
I don't want to stand, with the setting sun,
And hate myself for things I have done.

I don't want to keep on a closet shelf
A lot of secrets about myself,
And fool myself, as I come and go,
Into thinking that nobody else will know
The kind of a man I really am;
I don't want to dress up myself in a sham.

I want to go out with my head erect,
I want to deserve all men's respect;
But here in the struggle for fame and pelf
I want to be able to like myself.
I don't want to look at myself and know
That I'm bluster and bluff and empty show.

I can never hide myself from me;
I see what others may never see;
I know what others may never know,
I never can fool myself, and so,
Whatever happens, I want to be
Self-respecting and conscience free.

—Edgar A. Guest

Pleasure in Praising

I know of no finer way to make this a better place in which to live than to praise those who do worthy things. Both the giver and the receiver are blessed beyond words.

There is a vast difference between flattery and honest praise. The former disgusts, the latter lifts the spirit, like light turned on in a darkened room.

Honest praise never hurt anyone. It makes a better servant, employee, or friend. Without, many a servant, employee, and friend has been lost to the one most needing his service. We would all shrivel in usefulness and importance, both to ourselves and the world about us, without this praise given to us when deserved.

Most critics feel it more their duty to find fault than to praise. Many of them even become blind to all praise. A few years ago a play was started in a New York theater that every critic saw fit to condemn. Fortunately, the people who saw it liked it, told their friends about it—and the result was the longest run in the history of the theater at that time. It was clean, with plenty of laughs in it, and good entertainment. A play of such nature deserves praise. They are all too few.

A great and notable English editor—Sir W. Robertson Nicoll—wrote in one of his books that he never missed the opportunity to praise a young author, so long as he or she showed ability and wrote sincerely. He didn't believe in discouraging one because he hadn't become famous. Praise at the right time has helped to make many a man or woman, not only famous, but happily successful, which is more permanent.

Many a person has risen to great heights encouraged by a kind word of praise early in life. To give praise is the simplest service anyone can give—and it costs nothing but the effort.

TELL HIM NOW

If with pleasure you are viewing any work a man is doing,
    If you like him or you love him, tell him now;
Don't withhold your approbation till the parson makes oration
    And he lies with snowy lilies on his brow;
No matter how you shout it he won't really care about it;
    He won't know how many teardrops you have shed;   .
If you think some praise is due him now's the time to slip it to him,
    For he cannot read his tombstone when he's dead.

More than fame and more than money is the comment kind and sunny
    And the hearty, warm approval of a friend.
For it gives to life a savor, and it makes you stronger, braver,
    And it gives you heart and spirit to the end;
If he earns your praise—bestow it; if you like him let him know it;
    Let the words of true encouragement be said;
Do not wait till life is over and he's underneath the clover,
    For he cannot read his tombstone when he's dead.

—Berton Braley

TO A FRIEND

You entered my life in a casual way,
   And saw at a glance what I needed;
There were others who passed me or met me each day,
   But never a one of them heeded.
Perhaps you were thinking of other folks more,
   Or chance simply seemed to decree it;
I know there were many such chances before,
   But the others—well, they didn't see it.

You said just the thing that I wished you would say,
   And you made me believe that you meant it;
I held up my head in the old gallant way,
   And resolved you should never repent it.
There are times when encouragement means such a lot,
   And a word is enough to convey it;
There were others who could have, as easy as not—
   But, just the same, they didn't say it.

There may have been someone who could have done more
   To help me along, though I doubt it;
What I needed was cheering, and always before
   They had let me plod onward without it.
You have helped to refashion the dream of my heart,
   And made me turn eagerly to it;
There were others who might have (I question that part)—
   But, after all, they didn't do it!

—Grace Stricker Dawson

The Stuff

As so many of us have discovered—life is real and life is earnest and it is beset with obstacles and difficulties. Life is no bed of roses or bowl of strawberries.

This pilgrim journey is filled with responsibilities, toils, cares, pains, heartaches, failures, disappointments, detours, sorrow, and bereavement.

But for the stalwart noble ones there are innumerable compensations along the way.

There's the offer of love and laughter and a host of friendly companions to share the journey. And some will even lend strength when you are facing the fierce foes.

Joys come and satisfactions—when one faces his life's foes—endures their pressures and onslaughts—with head unbowed and character unsullied.

You can win if you have the right ingredients in your make-up—the stuff.

THE STUFF

The test of a man is the fight he makes,
  The grit that he daily shows,
The way he stands on his feet and takes
  Fate's numerous bumps and blows.
A coward can smile when there's naught to fear,
  When nothing his progress bars,
But it takes a man to stand up and cheer
  While some other fellow stars.

It isn't the victory after all
  But the fight that a brother makes,
The man who, driven against the wall,
  Still stands up erect and takes
The blows of fate with his head held high
  Is the man who'll win in the by and by,
For he isn't afraid to fail.

It's the bumps you get and the jolts you get
  And the shocks that your courage stands,
The hours of sorrow and vain regret,
  The prize that escapes your hands
That test your mettle and prove your worth,
  It isn't the blows you deal
But the blows you take, on the good old earth
  That shows if your stuff is real.

—*Author Unknown*

If I should win, let it be by the code
　　With my faith and my honor held high;
But if I should lose, let me stand by the road
　　And cheer as the winners go by.

—Author Unknown

From "ROOFS"

They say that life is a highway and its
　　mile-stones are the years,
And now and then there's a toll-gate
　　where you buy your way with tears.

It's a rough road and a steep road, and it
　　stretches broad and far,
But at last it leads to a golden Town
　　where golden Houses are.

—Joyce Kilmer

Life is not life at all without delight.

—Patmore

GIVE ME THE HEART OF A MAN

More than half beaten, but fearless,
    Facing the storm and the night;
Breathless and reeling, but tearless,
    Here in the lull of the fight,
I who bow not but before Thee,
    God of the Fighting Clan,
Lifting my fists I implore Thee,
    Give me the heart of a Man!

What though I live with the winners,
    Or perish with those who fall?
Only the cowards are sinners,
    Fighting the fight is all.
Strong is my Foe—he advances!
    Snapt is my blade, O Lord!
See the proud banners and lances!
    Oh, spare me this stub of a sword!

Give me no pity, nor spare me;
    Calm not the wrath of my Foe.
See where he beckons to dare me!
    Bleeding, half beaten—I go.
Not for the glory of winning,
    Not for the fear of the night;
Shunning the battle is sinning—
    Oh, spare me the heart to fight!

Red is the mist about me;
    Deep is the wound in my side;
"Coward" thou criest to flout me?
    O terrible Foe, thou hast lied!
Here with my battle before me,
    God of the Fighting Clan,
Grant that the woman who bore me
    Suffered to suckle a Man!

—John G. Neihardt

IT COULDN'T BE DONE

Somebody said that it couldn't be done,
  But he with a chuckle replied
That "maybe it couldn't," but he would be one
  Who wouldn't say so till he'd tried.
So he buckled right in with the trace of a grin
  On his face. If he worried he hid it.
He started to sing as he tackled the thing
  That couldn't be done, and he did it.

Somebody scoffed: "Oh, you'll never do that;
  At least no one ever has done it";
But he took off his coat and he took off his hat,
  And the first thing we knew he'd begun it.
With a lift of his chin and a bit of a grin,
  Without any doubting or quiddit,
He started to sing as he tackled the thing
  That couldn't be done, and he did it.

There are thousands to tell you it cannot be done,
  There are thousands to prophesy failure;
There are thousands to point out to you, one by one,
  The dangers that wait to assail you.
But just buckle in with a bit of a grin,
  Just take off your coat and go to it;
Just start to sing as you tackle the thing
  That "cannot be done," and you'll do it.

—*Edgar A. Guest*

40

Your Doubts

If you live by doubts they will handicap your success and usefulness. They will never make you a better person, or a more helpful friend, or a more useful citizen, or a more effective promoter of anything of worth.

People want beliefs, not doubts. Hence, Goethe declared: "Give me the benefit of your beliefs, if you have any, but keep your doubts to yourself, for I have enough of my own."

You may have a good friend, but when you begin to doubt his sincerity and become suspicious of his motives you create a chasm between you and the friend. If you doubt that you can do a particular job, you are likely not to do it at all. If you doubt that you will ever understand some people, you may close the door to all that is good, commendable, and fine about that person. Doubt is dangerous.

The attitude of the mind is all-important. If you doubt that your marriage will be successful, you will put forth little effort to make it work. If you doubt that your children will make anything out of their lives and tell them so, you may influence them to drift through life. If you doubt that life is your friend when you are in trouble, you bid for self-pity and give up. If you doubt that you are worth anything, you will tend to act as if you aren't.

> Our doubts are traitors,
> And make us lose the good we oft might win,
> By fearing to attempt.

—Shakespeare

41

No vision and you perish;
　　No ideal, and you're lost;
Your heart must ever cherish
　　Some faith at any cost.

Some hope, some dream to cling to,
　　Some rainbow in the sky,
Some melody to sing to,
　　Some service that is high.

—Harriett Du Autermont

Faith is to believe what we do not see,
and the reward of this faith is to see what we believe.

—St. Augustine

Give me wide walls to build my house of
　　Life—
The North shall be of Love, against
　　the winds of fate;
The South of Tolerance, that I may
　　outreach hate;
The East of Faith, that rises clear and
　　new each day;
The West of Hope, that e'en dies a
　　glorious way.
The threshold 'neath my feet shall be
　　Humility;
The roof—the very sky itself—Infinity.
Give me wide walls to build my house
　　of Life.

Be True

Lying is the most despicable of all crimes. The liar is the king of criminals. The last clean spot in a man's raiment turns crimson when he takes up the business of lying.

Truth is the highest thing a person can keep.

The heart of an honest man melts away almost unto death in the presence of the liar. The very mercy of a kind God blushes with bowed head in sadness at the sight and sound of the man who plies his lies. Scorned by society, the very soul of the liar revolts at the carrying about of bones and flesh so vile.

Truth is the highest thing a person can keep.

Recently a young man, large of mind and future, left his employment with a lie upon his lips. Coming into the seething whirl of the Great New York he sought his former friends. Immediately he began to hand out a stock of lies. More abominable than any abandoned thief he slyly exchanged lies for favors and for gold. Then nervously yet quietly sneaking away under cover of his lies, his soul naked of honor and character, he sought refuge under his own-made tent of lies. There self-convicted he now awaits judgment.

Truth is the highest thing a person can keep.

Mark Twain spoke more than humor when he said: "When in doubt, speak the truth." Nature itself closes its eyes in shame as the liar passes by.

Truth is the highest thing a person can keep.

You—young man, young woman, business builder, doer of good things—whoever you are, and in whatever groove

you work your way—listen! Starve and die, rather than lie.
Flee from the presence of a liar as from the plague. Grasp
the clean, strong hand of truth and follow its path through
the livelong hours of every single passing day.
Remember—truth is the highest thing a person can keep.

Never esteem anything as of advantage to thee that shall
make thee break thy word or lose thy self-respect.

—Marcus Aurelius

Dare to be true: nothing can need a lie;
A fault which needs it most, grows two thereby.

—Herbert

Truth, be more precious to me than eyes
Of happy love; burn hotter in my throat
Than passion, and possess me like my pride;
More sweet than freedom, more desired than
    joy,
More sacred than the pleasing of a friend.

—Max Eastman

Go, put your creed into your deed,
Nor speak with double tongue.

—Ralph Waldo Emerson

THE TRUE MAN

This is the sort of a man was he:
True when it hurt him a lot to be;
Tight in a corner an' knowin' a lie
Would have helped him out, but he wouldn't
    buy
His freedom there in so cheap a way—
He told the truth though he had to pay.

Honest! Not in the easy sense,
When he needn't worry about expense—
We'll all play square when it doesn't count
And the sum at stake's not a large amount—
But he was square when the times were bad,
An' keepin' his word took all he had.

Honor is something we all profess,
But most of us cheat—some more, some less—
An' the real test isn't the way we do
When there isn't a pinch in either shoe;
It's whether we're true to our best or not
When the right thing's certain to hurt a lot.

That is the sort of a man was he:
Straight when it hurt him a lot to be;
Times when a lie would have paid him well,
No matter the cost, the truth he'd tell;
An' he'd rather go down to a drab defeat
Than save himself if he had to cheat.

—Edgar A. Guest

Resist Resentment

Among the pesky parasites preying on a "little" mind, the most devastating to happiness is resentment. Often I've been robbed of inward peace and been made miserable by resentment.

Resentment is a form of jealousy, or a kinsman. We resent another's ability, calling it brass or gall; resent his success, calling it luck; resent his superb personality, calling it pretense—and so the pesky parasite goes.

We are made bitter, narrow, prejudiced, and downright ineffective by this costly indulgence.

Rout your resentment; run him out of your heart. Peace will return and active goodwill, and sincere appreciation for others. Yes, your soul will then prosper and be in health; fellowship will be restored, friendship resurrected.

Rout this robber, execute this parasite—only then may you find a truer peace of mind and the satisfying enlargements of a generous spirit. Just mix up a lot of love, and prayer, and effort—and yes, self-forgetting. Get more out of life: Get rid of your resentments.

The constant interchange of those thousand little courtesies which imperceptibly sweeten life has a happy effect upon the features, and spreads a mellow evening charm over the wrinkles of old age.

—*Washington Irving*

IF I HAD KNOWN

If I had known what trouble you were bearing;
What griefs were in the silence of your face;
I would have been more gentle, and more caring,
And tried to give you gladness for a space.
I would have brought more warmth into the place,
   If I had known.

If I had known what thoughts despairing drew you;
(Why do we never try to understand?)
I would have lent a little friendship to you,
And slipped my hand within your hand,
And made your stay more pleasant in the land,
   If I had known.

—Mary Carolyn Davies

If we give love and sympathy
   Even to those who hate us
We fill them so with mystery
   They know not how to rate us.

—Helen King

Life is too short to be little.

—Benjamin Disraeli

GIVING AND FORGIVING

What makes life worth the living
   Is our giving and forgiving;
Giving tiny bits of kindness
   That will leave a joy behind us,
And forgiving bitter trifles
   That the right word often stifles,
For the little things are bigger
Than we often stop to figure.
What makes life worth the living
   Is our giving and forgiving.

—Thomas Grant Springer

Duty

Duty is the idea by which we rob ourselves of the joy of work.

The pleasure of the soul is self-expression. Self-expression is found perfectly in work. Whoever has discovered his work has come upon the secret of happiness. That is, provided he does not spoil it all by calling it duty and making it drudgery.

Of course, one should do his duty and is entitled to his reward and praise. It is not that I would rob him of his deserts. Rather I am concerned because he is missing the finest element of his deserts.

Why not call it privilege, instead of duty? The one word connotes a banquet, the other a whip; one the chosen opportunity of a free man, the other the forced labor of a slave.

A soldier goes to war because it is his duty, but the best soldier, the one that gets the inner satisfaction of heroism, is the one who steps forward to volunteer for some enterprise of danger.

It's a wife's duty to take care of her children, to keep a home, and to make her husband happy; but she is not much of a success if a sense of duty is all that moves her, if she has not the inspiration of love that makes a woman glad to be a wife and mother.

Duty is iron. Privilege is golden.

The college boy whom his father compels to go to school, and who has only the feeling of duty to keep him at his books, is not going to get the good out of his opportunities that the boy gets who is working his way and looks upon school as an inestimable privilege.

Duty, unrelieved, made the hard Puritan.

Duty alone, makes the faithful clerk. But when it is lit up by a sense of opportunity, and the clerk transforms his duty by his enthusiasm, the first thing you know he owns the business.

Duty is stern. Privilege is joyous.

The great Teacher called on us to take His yoke upon us; but it was a transforming yoke; "Ye shall find rest," He added. When we put enthusiasm, vim, and interest in anything we have to do, work becomes play, labor becomes craftsmanship, duty smiles and is changed to opportunity.

Duty obeys the law. Privilege knows no law, but operates by love; and love is fulfilling the law. Duty, taken alone, is dead. The joy of doing comes from the emotions. Whatever we do without feeling, whatever is not the forthputting of soul energy, is second-rate. We are artisans, not artists. Duty is cold. And cold contracts. Duty, alone, makes life wintry and bleak.

Pour love into your work. Let the labor of your hands be the gestures of the soul, and you are carried up to the heights of genius by the exhilaration of the outflowing forces. What the nation needs is not merely a sense of patriotic duty, but an overwhelming passion to serve. No nation is safe without enthusiasm. Neither can anyone go far without it.

DUTY

To do your little bit of toil,
  To play life's game with head erect;
To stoop to nothing that would soil
  Your honor or your self-respect;
To win what gold and fame you can,
But first of all to be a man.

To know the bitter and the sweet,
  The sunshine and the days of rain;
To meet both victory and defeat,
  Nor boast too loudly nor complain;
To face whatever fates befall
And be a man throughout it all.

To seek success in honest strife,
  But not to value it so much
That, winning it, you go through life
  Stained by dishonor's scarlet touch.
What goal or dream you choose, pursue,
But be a man whate'er you do!

—*Edgar A. Guest*

The man who would lift others must be lifted himself, and he who would command others must learn to obey.

—*Author Unknown*

51

We are not sent into this world to do anything into which we can not put our hearts. We have certain work to do for our bread and that is to be done strenuously, other work to do for our delight and that is to be done heartily; neither is to be done by halves or shifts, but with a will; and what is not worth this effort is not to be done at all.

—*John Ruskin*

MY TASK

To be honest, to be kind;
To earn a little and to spend less;
To make upon the whole a family happier for his presence;
To renounce when that shall be necessary and not to be
    embittered;
To keep a few friends, but those without capitulation—
Above all, on the same grim conditions, to keep friends
    with himself—
Here is a task for all that a man has of fortitude and
    delicacy.

—*Robert Louis Stevenson*

GUILTY

I never cut my neighbor's throat;
   My neighbor's gold I never stole;
I never spoiled his house and land;
   But God have mercy on my soul!

For I am haunted night and day
   By all the deeds I have not done;
O unattempted loveliness!
   O costly valor never won!

—Marguerite Wilkinson

Words

That little tongue of yours, which you hardly ever look at, can be a beauty asset! In fact, it can make you one of the most fascinating of persons.

How does one display charm? By a pleasant manner, a pleasing wit, and by the words one speaks. Every word one utters either builds or destroys one's charm.

A person may have the reputation of being a wit, but he also may have the reputation of being catty, sarcastic, and mean. Then people do not think of him as being charming. They laugh at his wit and are entertained by it, but they avoid any intimate relationship with him—out of fear. No person wants to be criticized or subject to unfair gossip.

So watch your tongue. Make it build up your charm.

Just experiment saying the nice things instead of the mean things. Pay a sincere compliment to a person and watch him glow. How nice that a few lovely words can make a person feel happy!

There is a legend about a woman who had lost all her friends. She was miserable about her unpopularity and confessed this to a pastor and implored him to tell her how she could recapture the love of those she had alienated. He told her to take a feather pillow, release its stuffing to a high breeze and then begin to gather the feathers and put them back into the pillow.

The woman declared that was impossible. The pastor agreed and said it was just as impossible to make retribution for unkind words and deeds. An unkind remark is as a feather in the wind.

So say nice things, even to those who are nasty to you. In time, they will get their reward—just see!

In all of our human relations it is well to remember that the tone of our voice can completely change the meaning of our words.

I know a man, for instance, who can say the simple word "hello" over the telephone in such a warm and ingratiating way that every listener wants to meet him. I have known a girl who could murmur "Isn't it a lovely night?" with overtones in her voice that made you know the only answer she wanted to her question was a kiss.

A man can say "bad dog" in such a sympathetic tone that his pup will wag his tail, or "good dog" in such an angry fashion that the pup will cringe. The two words "go away" can be said so that they will convey the moods of fear, rage, arrogance, entreaty, despair, love, command. In other words, in our language, as in Chinese, tone is an important part of syntax, of meaning.

We often give offense, not so much by the thing we say as by the critical or combative tone in which we say it. So often we can win friends by nothing else but a friendly and sympathetic tone of voice.

So, watch your tongue. It can be your best beauty asset!

BRIDLE YOUR TONGUE

That speech—it hadn't been gone half a minute
Before I saw the cold black poison in it;
And I'd have given all I had, and more,
To've only safely got it back indoor
I'm now what most folks "Well-to-do" would call.
I feel today as if I'd give it all,
Provided I through fifty years might reach
And kill and bury that half-minute speech.
Boys flying kites haul in their white-winged birds,
You can't do that when you're flying words.
Careful with fire—is good advice we know:
Careful with words—is ten times doubly so.
Thoughts unexpressed may sometimes fall back dead,
But God Himself can't kill them when they're said.

—*Will Carleton, In "Farm Festivals"*

A Friend knocks before entering;
not after leaving.

THE TONE OF VOICE

It's not so much what you say
As the manner in which you say it;
It's not so much the language you use
As the tone in which you convey it;
"Come here!" I sharply said,
And the child cowered and wept.
"Come here," I said—
He looked and smiled
And straight to my lap he crept.
Words may be mild and fair
And the tone may pierce like a dart;
Words may be soft as the summer air
But the tone may break my heart;
For words come from the mind
Grow by study and art—
But tone leaps from the inner self
Revealing the state of the heart.
Whether you know it or not,
Whether you mean or care,
Gentleness, kindness, love, and hate,
Envy, anger, are there.
Then, would you quarrels avoid
And peace and love rejoice?
Keep anger not only out of your words—
Keep it out of your voice.

—*Author Unknown*

THE TONGUE

"The boneless tongue, so small and weak,
Can crush and kill," declares the Greek.
"The tongue destroys a greater hoard,"
The Turk asserts, "than does the sword."

A Persian proverb wisely saith,
"A lengthy tongue—an early death";
Or sometimes takes this form instead,
"Don't let your tongue cut off your head."

"The tongue can speak a word whose speed,"
The Chinese say, "outstrips the steed";
While Arab sages this impart,
"The tongue's great storehouse is the heart."

From Hebrew wit this maxim sprung,
"Though feet should slip, ne'er let the tongue."
The sacred writer crowns the whole,
"Who keeps his tongue doth keep his soul!"

—Author Unknown

True sincerity sends for no witnesses.

I'm careful of the words I say
To keep them soft and sweet;
I never know from day to day
Which ones I'll have to eat.

—*Author Unknown*

IT'S BETTER

It's better sometimes to be blind
To the faults of some poor fellow being,
Than to view them with visions unkind,
When there's good we ought to be
seeing.

It's better sometimes to be dumb,
Than to speak just to be criticizing,
Though it seems to be given to some
To recall traits both mean and de-
spising.

It's better sometimes to be deaf,
Than to hear only lying and pander,
For there's nothing so low as theft
Of a good name destroyed by slander.

—*Author Unknown*

Detours

Detours, roadblocks, and setbacks are very temporary. Don't let 'em hold you. Strike out on an untried way, it could well prove your best.

At times I've bruised my head trying to go through a blocked way. Drastic change comes along the way, but I would rather stay snug and secure in my old set routine — changing courses is terrifying. But when the first road block was met, I refused to fear and to weep and give way to bemoaning my luck. Weighing my worth, analyzing my abilities, I learned to set out on a new road in a different direction.

Dark seems the day of detour—doubt and gloom join our journey to plague and tempt us to self-pity and defeat.

'Tis then you need to recall that detours are temporary. There are other better roads, which pass through much challenge and excitement and whose destinations happen to be just the realm of your fondest dreaming.

Light—the vision of your distant dream—breaks through the temporary gloom, and you set your sights on this new goal and set out to achieve it.

FRIENDLY OBSTACLES

For every hill I've had to climb,
　For every stone that bruised my feet,
For all the blood and sweat and grime,
　For blinding storms and burning heat,
My heart sings but a grateful song—
These were the things that made me strong!

For all the heartaches and the tears,
　For all the anguish and the pain,
For gloomy days and fruitless years,
　And for the hopes that lived in vain,
I do give thanks, for now I know
These were the things that helped me grow!

'Tis not the softer things of life
　Which stimulate man's will to strive;
But bleak adversity and strife
　Do most to keep man's will alive.
O'er rose-strewn paths the weaklings creep,
But brave hearts dare to climb the steep.

—Author Unknown

Many a person has discovered that by bravely meeting difficult situations he has been pushed into accomplishing things which he never supposed he could do. Had Milton not been blind he probably would never have written much of his great poetry. John Bunyan's twelve tormenting years in Bedford jail afforded him the passion and the leisure to write *Pilgrim's Progress*. It was St. Augustine's sufferings that made possible his *Confessions*. Sickness and handicaps may mean that our careers will be thwarted in one way or another. Adversity may mean that we will witness our life's work reduced to ashes. Hardships may cause us to make detours, and detours are setbacks; but detours need not be defeats. They may prove to be opportunities!

—Author Unknown

To improve the golden moment of opportunity and catch the good that is within our reach is the great art of life.

—Johnson

The Cynic

He is extremely critical of others, calling them such things as egomaniacs, grasping crooks, limelight lovers, and plain no-good bums. When I'm with him ten minutes, I feel like I need a bath. So I shun him like I would the plague.

For it is down-right depressing to be in the presence of someone who sees no good in others. It is generally true that in lamblasting others, we echo our own secret faults. Psychologists say, "Allow any man to give free vent to his feelings about others, and then you may turn in perfect safety and say, 'Thou art the man.'"

Such a person is really revealing contempt for himself, but using others as a scapegoat. Real healing of his hateful personality will come only if he were to recognize his own faults. This humility would teach him to be tolerant and understanding of the motives and actions of the former victims of his destructive judgments.

"Confess your faults, one to another, that you may be healed."

A LITTLE WALK AROUND YOURSELF

When you're criticizing others,
And are finding, here and there,
A fault or two to speak of,
Or a weakness you can't bear;
When you're blaming someone's weakness,
Or accusing some of pelf—
It's time that you went out
To walk around yourself.

There are lots of human failures
In the average of us all;
And lots of grave shortcomings
In the short ones and the tall;
But when we think of evils
Men should lay upon the shelves
It's time we all went out
To take a walk around ourselves.

We need so often in this life
This balancing of scales;
This seeing how much in us wins
And how much in us fails
But before you judge another
Just to lay him on the shelf—
It would be a splendid plan
To take a walk around yourself.

—Author Unknown

To avoid trouble and insure safety, breathe through your nose. It keeps the mouth shut.

THREE GATES

If I am tempted to reveal
    A tale someone to me has told
About another, let it pass,
    Before I speak, three gates of gold.

Three narrow gates: First, is it *true?*
    Then, is it *needful?* In my mind
Give truthful answer, and the next
    Is last and narrowest, Is it *kind?*

And if to reach my lips at last,
    It passes through these gateways, three,
Then I may tell the tale, nor fear
    What the result of speech may be.

—Author Unknown

Anger

All poisons are not kept in chained bottles on drugstore shelves.

All the cases of strange illness and wasting are not due to subtle drops from India nor mysterious powders sold by old witches. And all the shocking deaths are not the result of taking tablets of bichloride of mercury thinking they are of aspirin.

The commonest, deadliest, and most dreadful of poisons are those we carry around with us. They are contained in our hearts. There is no doubt about the injurious effects of certain emotions upon the body. They are as well authenticated as the operation of henbane or arsenic.

The exudation of sweat glands, for instance, has been analyzed, and certain strong feelings have been shown to produce certain definite injurious secretions.

Not only the occasional outburst of anger, but those states we might call chronic anger, such as impatience, petulance, irritability, bad temper, and the like, produce clear forms of intoxication (poisoning) much like alcohol.

Many cases of chronic indigestion, nervousness, morbidity, and hypochondria can be attributed to slow anger poison. If one can clean harmful ferments out of his body by a dose of salts or by the use of bran and oil, he can also cleanse his system of far more toxic contents by forgiving his enemies every night before he goes to bed, by daily purging his consciousness of all hates, resentments, and grudges.

Anger is sometimes unavoidable, as when we witness or hear of some outrageous act of injustice or cruelty. But if we must have it, let it be quick and soon over. For when it remains in us it is we who suffer and not our adversary.

It unnerves our hands, blinds our vision, impairs our judgment, and when it leaps to vengeance invariably overleaps, bringing to us regret and remorse in lieu of satisfaction.

"Remember," wrote Lord Chesterfield, "there are but two procedures in the world to a gentleman and a man of parts; either extreme politeness or knocking down."

And mighty good advice it is from the old worldly-wise philosopher. For anger that is balked or impotent, if kept lurking in the mind, settles into a slow poison.

It distorts the features and makes even a handsome face ugly, gives a vicious twist to the smile and a forbidding cast to the eye. It distorts our thoughts, we become unpleasant companions to ourselves, and from ourselves there is no escape. It upsets sleep, disturbs the simple delights of eating and drinking, degrades our work, and spoils our play. I do not say, "Don't get angry," but "Don't stay angry."

YOU NEVER CAN TELL

You never can tell when you send a word
   Like an arrow shot from a bow
By an archer blind, be it cruel or kind,
   Just where it may chance to go.
It may pierce the breast of your dearest friend,
   Tipped with its poison or balm,
To a stranger's heart in life's great mart
   It may carry its pain or its calm.

You never can tell when you do an act
   Just what the result will be,
But with every deed you are sowing a seed,
   Though the harvest you may not see.
Each kindly act is an acorn dropped
   In God's productive soil;
You may not know, but the tree shall grow
   With shelter for those who toil.

You never can tell what your thoughts will do
   In bringing you hate or love,
For thoughts are things, and their airy wings
   Are swifter than carrier doves.
They follow the law of the universe—
   Each thing must create its kind,
And they speed o'er the track to bring you back
   Whatever went out from your mind.

—Ella Wheeler Wilcox

IN ANGER

When I have lost my temper
I have lost my reason too.
I'm never proud of anything
Which angrily I do.

When I have talked in anger
And my cheeks are flaming red
I have always uttered something
That I wish I hadn't said.

In anger I have never done
A kindly deed, or wise.
But many things for which I know
I should apologize.

In looking back across my life
And all I've lost or made,
I can't recall a single time
When fury ever paid.

—Schaber.

You can never have a greater or a less dominion than that over yourself.

—Leonardo Da Vinci

THE QUARREL

I quarreled with my brother.
I don't know what about.
One thing led to another.
Somehow we fell out.

The start of it was slight;
The end of it was strong.
He said he was right.
I knew he was wrong.

We hated one another.
The afternoon turned black
Then suddenly my brother
Thumped me on the back

And said, "Oh, come along,
We can't go on all night.
I was in the wrong."
So he was in the right.

—Eleanor Farjeon

RETALIATION

How often, for some trivial wrong,
   In anger, we retaliate,
We learn, although it takes us long,
   That life is far too brief for hate.

—Margaret E. Bruner

There is no old age for man's anger,
   Only death.

—Sophocles, Oedipus at Colonus

She built herself a little house
   All walled about with Pride;
Took Prudence as a servant,
   And locked herself inside.

"She drew the blinds down tight as tight
   When Sorrow chanced to roam.
Experience called—she sent down word
   That she was not at home.

"Then wherefore should she now complain
   And wherefore should she sigh,
That Life and Love and Laughter
   Have passed, unseeing, by?

—Author Unknown

Face It

Some people fancy that to dodge some work that they ought to do is about the easiest possible thing to do. The truth is, however, it is always easier to walk right up to your work and face it.

No one but laggards dig up excuses for dodging what they should face. It is unfortunate that the most costly lessons are many times learned late in life. The greatest reason for this is our timidity and cowardice in facing every problem just as soon as it faces us. Many a man has evaded a problem in his youth that he could have easily solved at that time and then gone on, but which he refused to grapple with until compelled to face it late in life under cover of the bitterest pangs of sorrow and remorse.

It takes greater courage to *decide* to do a thing, than it does to do the thing.

Have you a particularly difficult piece of work to do today? Face it. Have you an enemy? Face him—and make him your friend. You feel yourself capable of more important work than you are doing now? Face the new work and decide to master it. Whatever your problem, face it—with courage and without fear, and with the calmness that comes to a person when he decides to go ahead according to his own conscience and judgment.

Don't sidestep or dodge for anything. If a thing is worth working out, face it and finish it.

SEE IT THROUGH

When you're up against a trouble,
    Meet it squarely, face to face;
Lift your chin and set your shoulders,
    Plant your feet and take a brace.
When it's vain to try to dodge it,
    Do the best that you can do;
You may fail, but you may conquer,
    See it through!

Black may be the clouds about you
    And your future may seem grim,
But don't let your nerve desert you;
    Keep yourself in fighting trim.
If the worst is bound to happen,
    Spite of all that you can do,
Running from it will not save you,
    See it through!

Even hope may seem but futile,
    When with troubles you're beset,
But remember you are facing
    Just what other men have met.
You may fail, but fall still fighting;
    Don't give up, whate'er you do;
Eyes front, head high to the finish.
    See it through!

—Edgar A. Guest

JUST A MINUTE

I have only just a minute
Only sixty seconds in it,
Forced upon me, can't refuse it,
Didn't seek it, didn't choose it.
But it's up to me to use it,
I must suffer if I lose it,
Give account if I abuse it,
Just a tiny little minute—
But eternity is in it.

—*Author Unknown*

Kindness

The greatest lever to move the hearts of men is by acts of kindness. Kindness is the prime factor in overcoming friction and in making human machinery run more smoothly.

If a man, mistakenly, is your enemy, you cannot disarm him in any other way so surely as by doing him a kindly act.

Yes, if we are strong enough to do a kindness to someone who has wronged us, there is no more certain way of bringing about restitution than by an act of sincere kindness, either by word of mouth or by hand.

As Shakespeare would have said: "It is twice blessed— it blesses him that gives and he that receives." Further, the man who can overcome his frailties and prejudices toward another man who may have wronged him, increases his own moral and spiritual strength by rising above himself!

Kindness is one thing that you cannot give away: It always comes back!

> 'Tis the human touch in this world that counts,
>   The touch of your hand and mine,
> Which means far more to the fainting heart
>   Than shelter and bread and wine;
> For shelter is gone when the night is o'er,
>   And bread lasts only a day,
> But the touch of the hand and the sound of the voice
>   Sing on in the soul alway.

> —*Spencer Michael Free*

BEGIN TODAY

So brief a time we have to stay
Along this dear, familiar way:
It seems to me we should be kind
To those whose lives touch yours and mine.

The hands that serve us every day,
Should we not help them while we may?
They are so kind that none can guess
How soon they'll cease our lives to bless.

The hearts that love us, who may know
How soon the long, long way must go.
Then might we not their faults forgive
And make them happy while they live?

So many faults in life there are
We need not go to seek them far;
But time is short and you and I
Might let the little faults go by.

And seek for what is true and fine
In those whose lives touch yours and mine;
This seems to me the better way
Then why not, friend, begin today.

—Author Unknown

Life is short and we have not too much time for gladdening the hearts of those who are traveling the dark way with us. Oh, be swift to love! Make haste to be kind.

—Henri Frederic Amiel

Life is mostly froth and bubble;
  Two things stand like stone:—
Kindness in another's trouble,
  Courage in our own.

—Gordon

If I can stop one heart from breaking,
  I shall not live in vain;
If I can ease one life the aching,
  Or cool one pain,
Or help one lonely person
  Into happiness again
I shall not live in vain.

—Emily Dickinson

A LITTLE WORD

A little word in kindness spoken,
   A motion or a tear,
Has often healed the heart that's
     broken!
   And made a friend sincere.

A word—a look—has crushed to earth,
   Full many a budding flower,
Which had a smile but owned its birth,
   Would bless life's darkest hour.

Then deem it not an idle thing,
   A pleasant word to speak;
The face you wear, the thoughts you bring,
   A heart may heal or break.

—Author Unknown

I expect to pass through this world but once. Any good thing, therefore, that I can do or any kindness I can show to any fellow human being let me do it now. Let me not defer nor neglect it, for I shall not pass this way again.

—Stephen Grellet

THE HOUSE

I lived with Pride; the house was hung
With tapestries of rich design.
Of many houses, this among
Them all was richest, and 'twas mine.
But in the chambers burned no fire,
Though all the furniture was gold:
I sickened of fulfilled desire,
The House of Pride was very cold.

I lived with knowledge; very high
Her house on a mountain's side
I watched the stars roll through the sky,
I read the scroll of Time flung wide
But in that house, austere and bare,
No children played, no laughter clear
Was heard, no voice of mirth was there,
The House was high but very drear.

I lived with Love; all she possest
Was but a tent beside a stream.
She warmed my cold hands in her breast,
She wove around my sleep a dream.
And one there was with face divine
Who softly came when day was spent,
And turned our water into wine,
And made our life a sacrament.

—*William J. Dawson*

Accumulate Hope

Hope is heart—in full health. When hope begins to flicker away, beware.

Accumulate hope.

It is just as easy to become bankrupt in hope as to become bankrupt in money. Hope is a mixture. It is made up of equal parts of courage, work, will, and faith. Innoculate your system with these things and hope will hover about you, lead you on and defend you.

Accumulate hope.

Perhaps you are one of the people who measures hope in mere money, crude ambition, and flabby fame. Hope is not material. Hope is eternal, just like the stars. And if you are not digging away at a job that has an ever-living atmosphere to it, then change your job without delay.

Accumulate hope.

Hope brightens the eye, squares the jaw, and stiffens the backbone. Hope is the invisible picture of success. Hope, hope, hope. . . .

Accumulate hope.

TODAY MAY BE THE DAY

The morn is here. Today may be the day!
  Men go to rest each night with but a dream,
    That ere another nightfall may come true—
The brave explorer, the inventor gray,
  The seeker after nuggets in the stream,
    And all who plan and plod and dare and do.

The morn is here. Today may be your own!
  Up then with all the faith of all the past
    And carry on with all the vim of old—
Today your prow may touch a land unknown,
  Your mind discover what you seek at last,
    And in the dirt of labor gleam the gold.

The morn is here. Yea, you have sought for long,
  And seen night come, and still unfound the quest,
    Until the months, the years have rolled away;
But let this hope still keep your heart as strong
  As when the dream first stirred within your breast:
    The morn is here—today may be the day!

—*Douglas Malloch*

POWER OF HOPE

To suffer woes which Hope thinks infinite;
To forgive wrongs darker than death or
    night;
  To defy Power, which seems
    omnipotent;
  To love, and bear; to hope till Hope
    creates
From its own wreck the thing it contem-
    plates;
  Neither to change, nor falter, nor
    repent;
This, like thy glory, Titan, is to be
Good, great and joyous, beautiful and
    free;
This is alone Life, Joy, Empire, and
    Victory.

—Percy Bysshe Shelley

Everything that is done in the world is done by hope.

—Martin Luther

HOPE

He died!
And with Him perished all that men hold dear;
Hope lay beside Him in the sepulcher,
Love grew corse cold, and all things beautiful beside,
    Died, when He died!

He rose!
And with Him hope arose, and life and light.
Men said, "Not Christ, but Death, died yesternight."
And joy and truth and all things virtuous
    Rose, when He rose.

—Author Unknown

No vision and you perish;
    No ideal, and you're lost;
Your heart must ever cherish
    Some faith at any cost.

Some hope, some dream to cling to,
    Some rainbow in the sky,
Some melody to sing to,
    Some service that is high.

—Harriet Du Autermont

BE HOPEFUL

Be hopeful, friend, when clouds are dark and days are
    gloomy, dreary,
Be hopeful even when the heart is sick and sad and weary.
Be hopeful when it seems your plans are all opposed and
    thwarted;
Go not upon life's battlefield despondent and fainthearted.
And, friends, be hopeful of yourself. Do bygone follies
    haunt you?

Forget them and begin afresh. And let no hindrance daunt
    you.
Though unimportant your career may seem as you begin it,
Press on, for victory's ahead. Be hopeful, friend, and win
    it.

—Strickland Gillilan

The road winds up the hill to meet the height,
Beyond the locust hedge it curves from sight—
And yet no man would foolishly contend
That where he sees it not, it makes an end.

—Emma Carleton

Peace Within

You are tired of the turmoil? You want to escape the din and strife? You long for peace?

Then learn that the only peace that is full of rest, that means poise and calm energy, is inward peace.

The real peace may be found in the market-place, the hustings, the battlefield. There men strive and cry. There are smoke and dust, the hurrying messenger, the panting wrestler. But in the heart of the man who has found himself is the spot of calm.

On the contrary, one may be in a remote wilderness, "far from the maddening crowd's ignoble strife," alone with the twilight and the vast silences of nature, and yet be torn by the winds of passion or shaken by the thunders of fear.

A wise man will not seek peace without, but peace within. He will still the turbulence of desire, hold in leash the dogs of impatience, drive off the harpies of egoism, screen his soul from the mosquitoes of irritation, scotch the snakes of revenge, destroy the scorpions of self-pity, and with copious draughts of courage and pure faith ward off the fevers of fear, the chills of cowardice, the manias of superstition.

Peace! Peace within! Give me that, and let accusing tongues wag and envious hands tear, let the storms blow and the floods mount, and I shall be happy as a child in its mother's arms.

What deep wisdom and riches in the last words of the departing Teacher when He said: "Peace I leave with you, my peace I give unto you: Not as the world giveth, give I unto you. Let not your heart be troubled, neither let it be afraid."

CONTENTMENT

Money and fame and health alone
Are not enough for a man to own;
For healthy men are heard to sigh
And men of wealth go frowning by,
And one with fame may play his part
With a troubled mind and a heavy heart.
If these three treasures no joy possess,
How shall a man find happiness?

Health comes first in the famous three,
But cripples can smile, as we all must see;
Fame is sweet, as we all must own,
But the happiest hearts are not widely known.
Money is good, when it's truly earned,
But peace with fortune is not concerned,
For the bravest and loveliest souls we know
Have little of silver and gold to show.

Yet there must be a way to the goal we seek,
A path to peace for the strong and weak,
And it must be open for all to fare,
In spite of life's sorrows and days of care.
For those who have suffered the most the while
Look out on the world with the tenderest smile,
And those who have little of wealth to boast
Are often the ones that we love the most.

So I fancy the joy which men strive to win
Is born of something which lies within,
A strain of courage no care can break,
A love for beauty no thief can take—.
For they are the happiest souls of earth
Who gather the treasures of gentle worth—
The pride of neighbors, the faith of friends
And a mind at peace when the sun descends.

—*Edgar A. Guest*

'Till poverty knocked at her door
   She never knew how bare
The uneventful days of those
   Who have but want and care.

'Till sorrow lingered at her hearth,
   She never knew the night
Through which troubled souls might fare
   To gain the morning light.

'Till suffering had sought her house,
   She never knew what dread
Many wrestle with, or what grim fears
   Of agony are bred.

And yet till those unbidden guests
   Had taught her to possess
A clearer sight, she never knew
   The height of happiness.

—*Charlotte Becker*

God's Word

At the opening of New York's World's Fair in 1939, one of the most widely publicized stunts was the placing of the Time Capsule.

This was an eight-hundred-pound torpedo-shaped shell that Westinghouse Electric dreamed up and buried in Long Island to be dug up 5,000 years later. Into this capsule there was placed a host of miscellaneous modern articles—a Lily Dache hat, golf balls, and approximately ten million words of microfilmed matter.

Besides the published index of the contents of the capsule there was only one other book placed in it—the Bible. Westinghouse Electric stated, "The Bible of all books familiar to us today, will most likely survive through the ages. Therefore, the Bible we placed in the Time Capsule will be a sort of connecting link between the past, present, and future."

Voltaire said that in one hundred years the Bible would be an outmoded and forgotten book to be found only in museums. When the one hundred years were up, Voltaire's house was owned and used by the Geneva Bible Society. According to the latest American Bible Society report, the world has translated the Bible into 1,202 languages.

It is incumbent upon all of us however to translate it into life. The Bible is an instrument not an ornament; a chart, not a charm. Other books were given for our information, but the Bible alone was given for our transformation.

THE BIBLE! THERE IT STANDS!

Where childhood needs a standard
  Or youth a beacon light,
Where sorrow sighs for comfort
  Or weakness longs for might,
Bring forth the Holy Bible,
  The Bible! There it stands!
Resolving all life's problems
  And meeting its demands.

Though sophistry conceal it,
  The Bible! There it stands!
Though Pharisees profane it,
  Its influence expands;
It fills the world with fragrance
  Whose sweetness never cloys,
It lifts our eyes to heaven,
  It heightens human joys.

Despised and torn in pieces,
  By infidels decried—
The thunderbolts of hatred
  The haughty cynics pride—
All these have railed against it
  In this and other lands,
Yet dynasties have fallen,
  And still the Bible stands!

To paradise a highway,
    The Bible! There it stands!
Its promises unfailing,
    Nor grievous its commands;
It points man to the Savior,
    The lover of his soul;
Salvation is its watchword,
    Eternity its goal!

—*James M. Gray*

THE BIBLE

We search the world for truth. We cull
The good, the true, the beautiful,
From graven stone and written scroll,
And all old flower-fields of the soul;
And, weary seekers of the best,
We come back laden from our quest,
To find that all the sages said
Is in the Book our mothers read.

—*John Greenleaf Whittier*

And should my soul be torn with grief
   Upon my shelf I find
A little volume, torn and thumbed,
   For comfort just designed.
I take my little Bible down
   And read its pages o'er.
And when I part from it I find
   I'm stronger than before.

—Edgar A. Guest

THE BOOK OF BOOKS

Within this ample volume lies
The mystery of mysteries.
Happiest they of human race
To whom their God has given grace
To read, to fear, to hope, to pray,
To lift the latch, to force the way;
But better had they ne'er been born
That read to doubt or read to scorn.

—Sir Walter Scott